Finding
my
Way

GAYLE BRADSHAW

ISBN 978-1-64300-074-9 (Paperback)
ISBN 978-1-64300-075-6 (Digital)

Covenant Books, Inc.
11661 Hwy 707
Murrells Inlet, SC 29576
www.covenantbooks.com

Contents

Rising Up

The miracle of new morning
Has eased into my heart
Blessing me with
A brand-new start
God has brought
Fresh hope into my soul
As I step gingerly
Down a road I do not know
I believe
There is so much to come
Each passing moment
Is another battle won
Looking forward
Beyond what I can see
With dreams of all
I one day will be
I long for peace
It is almost in my grasp
Trying to separate this moment from my past
I'm reaching out
Life is more
Than pushing through the fear
It's plunging into a sea
Of all that I hold dear
I believe—
I choose to believe
As I step on

I'll find the strength I need
There is hope!
Fresh and new to me
Little by little
I am breaking free

Finding Faith

At times
Faith is difficult to grasp
Trying to separate
This moment from my past
My God
Gives me strength to push on
I struggle
My doubts and fears are not yet gone
But I believe
This fight is not the end
This moment—
I will step out again
I'm reaching
With all the hope in my heart
A new day
Is the chance for a new start
So…somehow…
I must make it through this day
Fighting desperately
But believing it will be okay
I have to—
I have to believe
If I keep pressing on
Someday I will be free
Learning…
And trying with all my might
I pledge today
I will not give up the fight

Beyond

I don't know the words to express
The hope I feel deep within
It's so far beyond
The places I have been
I believe
In what is to come
Feeling a sense of peace
With each battle that is won
I forgot I could actually feel joy
And I'm fighting to hang on
Afraid if I close my eyes
The joy will be gone
I've been trying so hard
To work through my fear
I have to hang on
For this moment the hope is here
I have to believe—I choose to believe—
There is so much life ahead
The struggle takes all my heart
In ways that can't be said
But I have come a long way
And I know there's a long road ahead
Feelings change and are scary
But I'm moving forward instead
I thank God for this moment
How good it feels right now
I'll keep on working

And keep my hands to the plow
Life really can be good
If I just believe
Holding on tightly
I've found the hope I need

Innocence Lost

Since ever so little
There has been no place to hide
Stripped of my body
Stripped of my pride
As I grew
Violated again and again
It's all I've ever known
It's all I've ever been
My adult life
Has been much the same
Raped and left
Feeling I'm the one to blame
When does it end?
Will I ever trust again?
I've nothing left
With which to defend
I feel naked
Even when I'm fully clothed
I look in the mirror
My own face I loathe
Did you hear me cry, Jesus?
Won't you throw me a line?
My body has been so used
It's never been mine
I give you this scarred body to you
I pray for your strength
And I pray one day...
You'll give me back my innocence

Turning This Around

I feel so lost
I don't know where to stand
But I'm trying to move forward
The best that I can
One moment has hope
The next in despair
I feel tormented
So difficult to bear
I don't know what to do
What is the next step?
How do I top the chaos
Going on in my head?
Trying so desperately
To know what is real
I cannot give in
To the desperation I feel
I must believe
Somehow I will get through
My emotions change so quickly
I don't know what to do
But I know deep down inside
There is hope to find
Struggling to grasp it
In this turmoil that is mine
Today is difficult
I'm reaching to God from within
Trying to escape

The way this day has been
But five minutes at a time
I will push on through
Trying to view
Each moment as new
Each moment a new chance
To reach beyond my thoughts
I know my God knows
How strongly I have fought
It will be okay
I cannot give in
I will keep on pushing
Until I'm able to win
There is hope
And I choose to believe
If I keep reaching out
I'll find the strength I need

Faith

What is faith?
The choice to believe…
Surrender my fear
To surrender my need
The desire…
To stand up and walk on
Though it seems
My strength is all but gone
I lay before God
My secrets—my heart
It is too late
To make a new start?
No matter
What rages inside
I simply cannot
Cease to try
I will step forward…
One foot then the next
I embrace all I can—
And I surrender the rest

Healing Has Begun

Feelings run bittersweet
I don't know the words to say
I have begun a healing—
I choose to live today
I've learned things
That I'll forever hold within
Stepping out
As I begin again
One step at a time
I'm finding my way
A new breath
is a new day
My hope extends so far
I truly do believe
If I keep on working hard
One day I will be free
The road has changed
Some things are new
Amazing twists and turns
One day I will be free
But my goals are within view
Hope graces my spirit
And faith my wounded heart
I am healing in so many ways
This is a brand-new start

Another Day

A flash of hope—
Where do I stand?
With some insecurity…
I reach out my hand
Embarrassed, but pushing on
Impulses torment my frame
But deep within flickers
A surviving flame
I'm struggling so
To overcome…
This rage inside
Is a tricky one
I can't get angry
At my past
Flashbacks—
Seem to converge fast
I'm torn about
What to believe
Searching desperately
For the courage I need
Have I
Let everyone down?
This battlefield
Is on some shaky ground
At times, I struggle
To know what is real
To break through

This terror I feel
I must not give up
Keep my head in the game
I'm fighting my self
It's the victory within I must claim
This is not the end
I'm frustrated—torn
I must hold on
Until God brings the morn
There is hope—
I must believe…
"Never say die…"
I'm down to my knees
One step at a time
I'll no longer hide
It feels impossible!
My spirit cries
I can do this
I will press on
My heart sometimes fails me
But trying to be strong
Here we are—
Another day
A little at a time…
I'm finding my way

God Help Me Believe

I'm a little confused—
Torn all apart
Here we are
Back at the start
I want to be strong
And keep pushing on
Where do I stand
When everyone is gone?
I'm longing for hope…
God, help me believe
I'm trying to step out—
Don't know what I need
I'm finding my way…
One step at a time
Face-to-face
With the turmoil in my mind
Confusion—uncertainty
I'm not always sure what is real
I don't understand
The despair that I feel
But I want to work through this
To feel hope in my heart
To trust in my God
When overwhelming fears start
I will not give up—
This is not the end
I may fall

But I get up again
I want to believe
In what lies ahead
Not all the memories—
I'll hold on instead
If only I could trust
There is so much to come
Today's a new day
Another battle won
I will move forward
Though I can't clearly see
I'll give God all my heart
And be all I can be

Moving Forward

My biggest fault
Is my failure to believe—
Battling with myself—
Longing to be free
My feelings change so much
From one moment to the next
Trying so desperately
To find an inner rest
My thoughts become jumbled—
Uncertain and confused—
But I have discovered
A hope that's fresh and new
I'm trying to maintain
A faith that will last
To believe in what lies ahead
Not my gripping past
I don't really understand
What is going on
But trying to press on—
Trying to be strong
I have such a battle with impulses—
Struggling for control
I cry out to my God…
Cry out with everything I know
I'm moving forward
Pressing on
Trying to believe

That soon will come the dawn
I cannot base my thoughts
On the distress that I feel
The conflict in my mind…
My fight to know what's real
This is a new day—
A new hour
My God has brought to me
A song of strength and power
There is hope
I'm committed to the path I'm on
I'm still battling myself
But the hopelessness is gone

Letting Go

Thrown about
Caught in despair
The pain in my heart
Almost more than I can bear
So overwhelming
It caused my heart to burn
My relief feels more
Than I could ever earn
I searched my soul
Looking for peace
Somehow some help
In my time of need
I came to my God
Laid it all at his feet
And a little at a time
He's setting me free
I let go of the hurt
And surrender my pain
Climbing out of the pit
That has kept me restrained
There is hope!
Breaking free from the chains—
God's brought life—
His mercy reigns

A Change

I may not understand
All that I feel
Sometimes I don't know
What is real
But there has been
A change deep within
Putting some distance between
Here and the places I've been
I have found hope
A reason to go on
Even in distress
That hope is not gone
I feel a strength
I do not understand
But I know deep within
It is in God's hands
In confusing pain
In the middle of distress
There is a way to life—
Somehow nothing less
I can endure
Anything I feel
Without acting on it
A new path that is real
I may not know
What step comes next
But in the middle of despair

My God brings me rest
I am finding life
When it feels difficult to go on
The chains have been broken
The hopelessness is gone

The Journey

My spirit is at a loss
My heart feels it's been crushed
It feels like I cannot hold on
But I know that somehow I must
What is it I feel?
I don't understand
Slipping further
Into a sea of dry sand
Slipping further
Deeper yet still
Want to hang on
But I can't find the will
How do I hope?
What is it I'm doing wrong?
My heart has failed me
And the journey's so long
What is hope?
How do I believe?
I'm' reaching out to God
For the strength that I need
What next?
Each moment seems so long
Fighting with all my might
To be brave and strong
My most difficult battles
Are with myself
A despair deep within

Words simply do not tell
But I have not given up
I will not cease to fight
Pushing on with all my strength
Breaking through the night
There is hope on the horizon
Just outside my grasp
Searching to find peace
A true peace that will last
It's hard to believe
In what lies ahead
Not curl up and hide
But step out instead
I will not stop until I get a grip
On hope, on faith, on peace
And destroy the silent roar
Of depressions inner beast
Because there is hope
And there are second chances
One day I will again dance
I will hang on
No matter what comes my way
Inching forward
Until I find a new day

Here Is My Hand

Come to the mountain
And take my hand
Surrender yourselves
And settle into my plan
You're coming from
So many situations in your life
Trust in my word
And quit asking me why
I have brought you to this place
For a reason
This—a new season
My love for you abounds
So deeply from my heart
Surrender your pain
Today's a new start
Join hands with your sisters
Let my love flow
What lies ahead
Is so much greater than you know
Do you feel my hand?
Let go of yesterday
Let your spirit be renewed
I am here for you
Feel my warm protection
Put your trust shoes on
And join in the run
This day's a new day

Accept the strength of my hand
Let's walk on forward
For this is my plan

On the Path

Sometimes I lose track
Of the path I am on
Times of despair—
But trying to be strong
I come to my God
Lay it all at his feet
He brings light
In my time of need
At times I fear
What this day will bring
Bouts of confusion
And doubts that ring
I may struggle
Bu this is not the end
I am in God's hands
And my heart is on the mend
I believe
In what is yet to come
I'm moving forward
This day a battle won
I'm excited
About today
I feel more hope
Than my words can say
I even feel joy!
What is happening?
As I press forward

My heart just sings
I didn't expect
This renewing of hope
M spirit is free
My heart is full
This very moment
Is a fresh start
Strongholds inside
Are coming apart
Moving on—
Here we go!
Stepping out
In this peace that just grows
I'm so thankful
As I face this day—
Step by step…
I'm finding my way

In the Heart

Waiting for the dawn
From a deep, dark night
It feels impossible
But I won't give up the fight
What now?
I've been struggling so much
For so very long
I've ached for true hope's touch
How can I learn to fly?
When it takes all for just one step
So much turmoil in my heart
And confusion in my head
I feel so insane
What is real?
I can't make sense
Of the emotions I feel
But I will break through
Keep pushing on
Trusting someday
The despair will be gone
To see the light before the end…
How much faith does that take?
I have little strength left
Before my spirit breaks
But somewhere deep inside
I believe
God will bring the His grace

To meet my inner needs
If I could just trust
And hang on tight
I will keep moving forward
I will make it through the night
I choose to live
I choose to believe
Even though I'm afraid
And I'm not sure what I need
I'm going to trust
Even when I don't feel any faith
Calling out to my God
I'll break free from this place
I choose to keep on figuring
I choose to believe good
Even when I feel alone
And I don't feel understood
I pledge to push on
Things are going to change
Though it's unfamiliar territory
And it feels a little strange
I must persevere through this night
Tomorrow is another day
I may not understand
But life is here to stay

Longing for Love

To be loved…
If I could believe
If only—
That would ever be
I look in the mirror
And long to cry
Can't forgive myself
No matter how hard I try
Forgive myself
For the uncertainty
The confusion and the shame
So much time has passed
Yet the shame remains
I don't know who I am
I long to be loved
And long to understand
To somehow rise above
I do not like myself…
Where do I go from here?
How do I make it through
The overwhelming fear?
I do not know
What love is all about
Trapped inside myself
Is there a way out?

Amazing

It's amazing
How things work out
When you're struggling with your fears
And your own self-doubts
Some moments feel impossible...
No way to make it through
The confusion and uncertainty...
The turmoil that is you
But I am on a path
And though I can't see the way
I step forward
And make it through the day
I cry out to my God...
I can't control when He brings peace
But when I least expect it—a reason to go on—
I receive the breath of life I need
Trust is not easy
It is a process—
Choosing to believe
And push through every pain and test
There is hope—
When I feel I can't go on
Down a path I do not know...
Somehow God brings a song
I trust Him
To bring me through—
Through the darkness of night

To a day that is new
I accept the challenge…
To not simply "survive"
But work toward being a "victor"
And be thankful for my life

Fighting On

I'm struggling with my heart
Pierced with despair
Tomorrow is coming
And it feels more than I can bear
I can't find the words to explain
The confusion and uncertainty
But I call out to God
And it brings me to my knees
I may not understand
Lost within my own thoughts
But as the day goes on
Comes faith in my heart
Peace may be hard to find
But I truly believe
If I can just hold on
I will find the strength I need
I know there is hope
For I feel a spark
Handling it tenderly
I'm holding it close to my heart
I believe
I am moving on
Even if the despair is not totally gone
It will be okay
Pushing forward
Determined—
Mindful of all I'm fighting for

There is life ahead
I am stepping on
I will fight with all my might
The hopelessness is gone

Secrets

Sharing the secrets
The pain within
Feels like
An unforgivable sin
It is a weakness
To uncover my heart?
Embarrassment—shame—
Are such a large part
Others will doubt
The effort I make
But reaching out…
For hope to awake
There is more to me
That what I fight
Then flashbacks make
The daytime like night
More than the struggle
To understand all that is me
My overwhelming self-doubt
That brings me to my knees
I try so hard
To use the skills I've learned
But my mind is confused
Don't know which way to turn
Impulses torment…
And voices confuse
Moments of clarity

And peace are too few
Help me, God,
What am I doing wrong?
Pushing on...
I want so much to be strong

I Will Overcome

Sometimes words
Are so difficult to find
Trying to express
What's on my heart and mind
I've been struggling
Reaching for hope
Trying to live
All that I know
Working just to
Make it through the day
Please, dear God,
Won't you show me the way?
Where do I
Go from here?
Pushing hard…
Pushing through the fear
I choose life
I choose to believe
I believe
One day I'll be free
I won't give up
No matter what I feel
At times
Not even sure what is real
I feel pain
So deep within
I cannot allow

The uncertainty to win
The present somehow lives
The past is dead
I want to believe
In what lies ahead
To learn
To dance in the rain
There's much to overcome...
But there's so much to gain

The VA

Where do all the old soldiers go?
The men who have sailed—
The airmen who've flown—
The marines who have marched—
How many miles?
We come here from time to time
For an uplifting word, a smile
Here to heal
To receive precious care
To be reminded of the bonds
That we all still share
Brothers and sisters
United as one
For they understand
When all's said and done
The wars we've been through
Battle in our hearts and our minds
Sometimes coming home
Brings a sense of peace we can find
We've given our all
In self-sacrifice
And for the deeds we have done
We're still paying the price
We love this land
It's what we stand for
And with your help
We'll try to give more

Here—the VA—
Our port in the storm
A healing balm
For hearts that still burn

Beginning to Change

It can be so confusing...
Yet I know which way to turn
I ask God to teach me to apply
All that I have learned
I have to believe the good
Despite what I may feel
Even when I'm afraid
And I'm not even sure what is real
I believe—
In what is yet to come
Though I may get overwhelmed
At the race I've still to run
I will not give up
I trust God with my heart
I have begun to change...
This is just the start
Turning over my thoughts...
Sometimes over and over again
I cannot allow my present
To be dictated by where I've been
There are moments—
Surrendering the pain inside—
When I'm afraid and tempted
To curl up and hide
But I am reaching out
I am pushing on...
There are difficult times

But my hope is not gone
It's not gone
because I believe…
I believe
In more than what I can see

Morning

There are times
When the joy is not there
I come to God
And lay my heart bare
I cannot focus
On just what I feel
God has supplied
A hope that is real
Even when I struggle
He gives grace to me
Stepping out
On a road I can't see
I believe
He will bring me through
After a night of conflict
This morning is new
Circumstances
Are hard to understand
But in the midst of turmoil
I see His hand
Pushing on—
I believe—I believe!
I believe
In more than I see
I trust the Almighty
Growing each day
In spite of confusion

I'm finding my way
The strongholds
Are coming apart
Moving forward
Today's a new start

I Won't Break

My life is coming together
In ways I did not foresee
Little by little
I am breaking free
Finding ways
To live what is in my heart
Every day—every hour—
A new start
There are moments
I have to fight with all my being
But I push through the desperation
And my spirit begins to sing
There is more to life
Than struggling with its pain
More than the moments of darkness
Learning there is much to gain
I may bend—
But I won't break
When I believe in life
My spirit wakes
I pledge to press on
No matter what it is that comes
Even if I have battles
I have hope enough
Trusting there is strength
Someday—
I'll be all I long to be

Do You See My Heart

Do you see my heart?
Do you hear my cry?
I need the strength to stay alive
I feel lost
Don't know the way
Trying desperately
To push on through this day
I feel like giving up
My heart aches deep inside
I want to pull within
Curl up and hide
I don't feel any hope
I don't understand how I feel
Thoughts and angry voices
Not sure what is real?
My spirit is beaten down
It hurts so in my heart
Confusion and uncertainty
Are ripping me apart
I'm not sure of my next step
Which way do I go?
I have no faith—
What next? I just don't know…
Hanging on with both hands

In Shadows

It's dark
Can't see my way
Not much difference
Between night and day
It's all shadows
A compromising gray
Long to speak
But no words to say
In a tomb
Of dampness and death
Full of all
The tears I have wept
How can I escape
These prison walls?
I step forward
But quickly fall
Unsure of
My very next breath
Lost my footing—
What happens next?
Trying to believe
In what I can't see
I cry out—
Here on my knees
Are you there, God?
Please be near to my heart
My heart aches—

Torn all apart
I ask
What must I do?
For you to hear—
To be close to you
Here's my life
I surrender it all
What now?
Lord, it's your call

Hands to the Plow

When it's hard to understand
What I'm going through
Struggling to rise above
And options seem few
I surrender to my God
My distress and pain
Again—a new beginning
There is so much to gain
I simply have to trust
And apply all I have learned
Trust in His healing power—
My whole world takes a turn
Anytime—any moment
Is the time for a fresh start
Feeling now some purpose
As He comforts my heart
My hands to the plow—
Gradually moving ahead
Not caught up in my thoughts…
Finding peace instead

My Fiftieth Birthday

Today is a day
Of reflection and prayer
Trying to understand
My life—my cares
Turning fifty has brought
Thoughts pouring through my mind
I'm not sure exactly
What I hope to find
I expected something different
At this point in life
I can't turn the clock back
Or answer all the "whys"
Today I really cried
For the first time in years
I didn't shut it down
I found relief in my tears
In fifty years
I have seen many trials
In storm of confusion
Reaching for hope all the while
My heart is wounded
But this is not the end
Trying to draw wisdom
From the places I've been
I'm not giving up
Looking to the life ahead
Feeling a mixture of pain

But choosing hope instead
This is a new day
Which means a new chance
My spirit is working
Toward finding life's dance
I may not feel great strength
But I choose to believe
Reaching out in faith
For the support that I need
Today may have been
A difficult day
But I will press on
I step forward as I pray
I'm feeling hope
There is real life still to come
One hour at a time
This day is won
My heart is revived
No matter what I feel
I'll never cease to try
In the hours ahead
Will come a new day
A little at a time
Still finding my way

I Feel Lost

I feel lost
I don't know where I stand
Fighting for some peace
With everything I can
My body is not safe
Each time that I turn
It happens all over again
Hope and honor just burn
I am afraid—
It feels so deeply real
Stringing me along…
The overwhelming confusion I feel
How do I separate
This moment from my past?
How do I move forward?
And find a strength that will last?
Stepping forward
Searching for hope within
So overwhelmed
Fighting to keep my last bits of innocence

Dear God, It's Me Again

I do not understand, God
But I am trying to believe
The battle is so intense
Where is the faith I need?
I question my own existence
I question what is real
Somehow help me conquer
This desperation that I feel
It's so very overwhelming...
My heart cries out to You—
One moment at a time—
That's all that I can do
I was feeling so much better...
More at peace with myself
A matter of hours
And thrown right back into hell
I cannot allow myself to believe
The voices—all the lies
I'm trying to remember
You're right here at my side...
My spirit aches
From the voices and the thoughts
I know that you know, my God
How very hard I've fought
Please accept my prayer
Help me find peace of mind
I'm trying to have hope...

Not be the quitting kind
As much as I may long, at times,
To throw it all away
I'm struggling to be strong
And defeat that need to pay
You've brought me this far...
And I believe in You—
You're at work in my life
Even when I haven't a clue
In a matter of a few seconds
My world gets turned around
Images that torment...
Sensation...sounds
I will keep on fighting—
For you've given me hope again
I trust you to redeem my soul
From the places I have been

Hope Found Me

I found peace
In the darkness of night
Hope rescued me
From deep in the fight
Relief from despair
And uncertainty
The next step
Was so very hard to see
It felt impossible…
I couldn't see the way
My heart was unsure
But I found a new day
I will push on
I choose to believe
A little at a time
God is setting me free
There is hope

No Matter What It Takes

My spirit cries out—
Where do I stand?
I've fallen so short
Of the life I had planned
Anxiety encompasses
My entire being
Overwhelmed by the battles
Each day brings
I'm at a loss…
What am I doing wrong?
Trying so hard
To have faith and be strong
Confusion eats
Through my spirit's core
It's so hard not to give up
Hard to fight anymore
But deep inside
There's a tiny flicker of hope
Though I don't know how to grasp it
Or which way to go
But I'm trying to believe
There are better days ahead
Even though I've lost strength
And my faith is all but dead
I may bend—
But I won't break
No matter what it takes

A new step is painful
I'm unsure what to do
But one moment at a time
I will push through
Nothing is impossible
If I can just believe
There's so much I long to do
And so much I want to be
If I choose life
Then that's reason enough
I will put my trust
In my God above
One day at a time
One step to the next
As I surrender my fears
I'm finding rest
I pledge today
With all of my might
I will push on
Never give up the fight
Trusting my life
In God's strong hands
Using coping strategies
And developing a plan
I am excited
With these words I have said
Moving on
There's so much life ahead

I Don't Understand

I don't understand where I'm at—
The things that I feel
The thoughts, the fears, the voices
How do I know what is real?
I'm not sure of the present
What I believe
What triggers the confusion?
What triggers my need?
I long for someone to understand
For someone to hear my cry
I have to learn to trust
Before the last of my hope dies
How can I come to terms with my past?
How can I come to terms with today?
I can't understand myself
And it's difficult to find my way
I pray God can see my heart
And forgive my uncertainty
There's so much I long to do
And so much I long to be

Where Do I Stand

Searching for
Where I stand
Where I'm going
Where I've been
The past is past
Trying to let it go
Amazed at today—
The hope I have known
Reaching out
Reaching for peace
Far beyond
What I can see
Today is a gift
From God to my soul
He's bringing me healing
And making me whole
The hope
That I have felt today
Is bringing me through—
I'm finding my way
I have found
New life within
So far beyond
The roads I have been
At times I'm afraid
Of what tomorrow will bring
But moving forward—

Trusting my King
It doesn't matter
How many times I have failed
God can still
Cause my spirit to sail
My fears
To Him I bring
My anxiety I surrender
And my heart starts to sing
Pushing on
It's a new day
I am growing
And peace finds its way
Reaching forward
To what is to come
Finding joy
This life is the one

A Change

I may not understand
All that I feel
Sometimes I don't know
What it is that's real
But there has been
A change deep within
Putting some distance between
Here and the places I've been
I have found hope
Reason to go on
Even in distress
That hope is not gone
I feel a strength
I do not understand
But I know deep within
It is in God's hands
In confusing pain
In the middle of distress
There is a way to live—
Somehow nothing less
I can endure
Anything I feel
Without acting on it
A new path that is real
I may not know
What step comes next
In the middle of despair

My God brings me rest
I am finding life
When it feels difficult to go on
The chains have been broken
The hopelessness is gone

To Be Understood

I don't understand where I'm at
Or what I'm going through
Can't seem to grasp the hope—
I'm unsure what to do
I don't want to let anyone down
I don't want to fail this time
I'm struggling so much with confusion
And turmoil in my mind
Trying to distract myself
And focus on something good—
Not sure how to explain—
I don't feel understood
Where are the words
That can speak my heart?
The desperation
That is ripping me apart
I feel despair
I'm trying to turn it around
The urges that torment
And somehow keep me bound
I'm not giving up
No matter what I feel
I have a spirit of determination
That nothing in this world can steal
I feel so inadequate
God, please help me be strong
I will not give up—
I will keep pressing on

Maze

Words don't come easy
For the pain in my heart
Trying to find the truth
Is ripping me apart
I call out to my God
For I don't know the way
Something inside must change
If I'm to make it through this day
I do not deserve
For anyone to care
Can I believe I'm loved…
Do I even dare?
Because if I believe
It will get turned around
And my search for hope and peace
Become so tightly bound
Confusion, fear, uncertainty
Brew in my spirit's core
A maze of twists and turns
And I cannot find the door
Is there new life to come?
I want so desperately to know
I want to move forward
Please show me the way to go
I will keep on fighting
I will not give in
I want to separate the present

From the places I have been
I'm afraid—very afraid
But I choose to believe
I know I've made mistakes
I don't even know what I need

At a Loss

Despair eats at my core
I simply cannot bear any more
What is it I am living for?
My God, where are you?
Help me, please
The pain in my heart
Brings me to my knees
What is it that
You want from me?
I cry out and cry out
Why won't you set me free?
I don't understand…
What am I doing wrong?
Help me hold on
Help me be strong
I don't even know
How to believe anymore
My world spins round and round
Please help me find the door
I have to hang on, God
Please take my hand
I'm fighting
With everything I have
I need hope
In my overwhelmed heart
If there's a way
Show me how to start

I'm willing to work
I'm willing to fight
But right now
Feels like an endless night
Walking one step at a time
Walking without sight
All I ask
Is that you bring me to the light
There is a snatch of hope
Deep down it lays
Can it overcome
All the mistakes I have made?
Give me hope
And I will press on
I will surrender the pain
Until You bring the dawn
I pledge to not give up
Not to give in
Take me far away
From the places I've been
I am beginning to hope
I can change this day
If you'll fuel my spirit, dear God
I will finish the race

Believe

What does it mean to change...
Is it about what I believe?
Choosing what I do with my thoughts...
Trusting what I cannot yet see
Having faith—
Despite the power of what I feel
Even when my mind is confused
And I'm not sure what is real
How do I believe?
How do I press on?
If I hold on with all my might
Will morning bring a fresh new dawn?
Dear God Almighty,
I come to you
Heal my heart and spirit
Teach me to walk in a way that is new
Give me hope—help me work
Toward peace with myself
Not just thoughts and words—
Help me to live it well
It's never too late
To begin again
I will not continue to allow my future or present
To be dictated by where I've been

From Deep Within

Drawing hope
From deep within
Gaining strength
From where I've been
I have
Come a long way
Feeling relief
From that need to pay
Today I had
Moments of desperation
I fought with all my heart
And it's another battle won
My soul is healing
My spirit is coming alive
I'm no longer searching
For all the reasons why
Tonight, reaching out
To someone else
Has brought me out
Of the panic I felt
This is just the beginning
But I'm starting to grow
The more I choose to believe good
The more peace I know
I must choose
Not to act on my fears
But allow myself to be human and allow the tears

Then let it go
When I share how I feel
Take chances
And be honest and real
There's life ahead
Joy and hope yet to find
As I work through
What's on my heart and my mind
I'm beginning to think
It's going to be okay
Starting again and again
Every day's a new day

Working through the Fear

It's a difficult job
Working through the fear
When I feel unsure
And the way is just not clear
I step into each moment
Still afraid of what it brings
Second to second—
The outcome not yet seen
I'm frightened of myself…
The compulsions that come
With precious relief
With each battle that is won
I cannot stop these drives
Though I try with all my might
It's up and down and back and forth
But I will not give up the fight

Choice

Struggling with thoughts
To throw it all away
I need the pain to ease
If I'm going to make it through this day
It's a nonlinear path—
So they say
It sure has been
Back and forth today
What am I doing wrong?
Why am I so afraid?
How can I build
On the steps that I have made?
It hurts deep within
I don't know which way to turn
I need to learn to live
All the things that I have learned
My God, give me strength
Help me to believe
Refresh my dreams
Give me the hope I need
I come to you…
I'm listening for your voice
No matter what comes my way
Let life always be the choice

A New Day

Well…a new day
Here we go!
Learning new things
As I begin to grow
I feel so hopeful
It's flooding my heart
One step at a time
It's a new start
Forgetting yesterday
It will be okay
Excited about today
Beyond what words can say
I believe!
Pushing on
Enjoying the peace
That came with this dawn
I'm trusting my God
As I move ahead
Truly believing
The words I have said
I'm stepping out
As gently as I pray
Looking forward
It's a New Day!

Whatever Comes

I'm finding hope
For my burdened heart
The thoughts binding me
Are falling apart
Having faith
For whatever may come
Each hour I live
Is another war won
Doing more
Than just getting by
Breaking through
All the questions why
Finding peace, finding hope
A new strength within
Moving forward from
The dark places I've been
I believe
There is real life ahead
When fear hits my head
I push on instead
It's a new start
It's a new day
One day at a time
I'm finding my way

Survive

Where my mind goes
I don't quite understand
Trying to bring together
Heart, head, and hands
But I can do this—
No matter what I feel…
At times, though,
I'm not sure what is real
Desperately using
All the skills I've been taught…
It's so difficult—
Sorting my thoughts
I do believe—
I am being transformed…
Walking carefully
On through the storm
I cannot give way
To emotions that surge,
To thoughts that torment…
They smother my courage
I can learn from my past
And whatever is today
Little by little…
I am finding my way
I feel hope within
I will do more than "survive"
Here's my spirit and heart—
One day I will "thrive"

Searching

My heart is heavy
But I cannot cry
The moment feels impossible
But I will not cease to try
I do not understand
All that's going on
I want so very much
To have faith and be strong
I bring to God
My wounded heart
And the harassing demons
That are ripping me apart
I'm confused and afraid
Struggling deep within
Searching for hope...
Where do I begin?
It's difficult to trust—
To share what's going on inside
To share my secrets...
It's tempting just to hide
Trying—
Trying to push beyond
Believing—
That soon will come the dawn
Taking chances—
I know I must manage my distress
But right now
I'm more afraid of life than I am of death

Hope Begins with a Choice

I'm preparing for tomorrow
And I choose to believe
I believe
In more than I can see
Stepping out—
It's a new day
Some uncertainties…
But I'm finding my way
A little at a time
I'm pushing on
A bit afraid
But moving along
It's difficult to know
What to expect
I question myself…
What happens next
I'm stronger than
The fear that I feel
Holding onto a flicker
Of hope that is real
Surrendering my doubts
To take a new step
Giving my best
And meeting each test
In the moments that
My hope can't be found
Somehow my faith keeps me

On firm, solid ground
Looking forward
To what lies ahead
Putting my past
Failures to bed
I don't have to repeat
My many mistakes
I won't give up
No matter what it takes
Hope begins with a choice
Despite what I may fear
Hanging on with both hands
A hope I pray will soon be real
In my service in the marines—
Nothing felt impossible
A soul overflowing
A heart that was full
This moment I commit my heart
To reach beyond what I can see
Stretching forward—
I know one day I will be free

With All of My Might

Pushing forward
With all of my might
I don't quite understand
But I'm deep in the fight
My emotions change so much
From one moment to the next
Struggling and searching
For a moment of rest
Trying to face myself—
Hardest thing I've ever done
Then a new challenge rages
With each battle that is own
I have not a chance
To recover from the night
So I reach out again
And grasp the hope with all my might
One more step

Moving Beyond

Trying to find hope
But where do I start?
A battle between
My mind and heart
I'm struggling desperately
To find inner peace
I've failed many times
But there's so much I long to be
I want to have Faith
I want to Believe
This fortress surrounding me
I'm reaching deep within
For that hope to go on
Trying to determine
What I'm doing wrong
Hope can be evasive
Faith hard to grasp
But little by little
I'm letting go of my past
It's confusing—
I feel like I don't know myself
But I have a drive inside
That words cannot tell
It's going to be okay
Step by step—pushing on
If I hold on tight
Each night becomes a dawn

I'm reaching out to God
He comforts my heart
Even when my heart is in pain
Each day is a new start
So what does that mean
When despair torments my soul?
I'm making a choice
Climbing from within the deepest hole
Choosing to believe Good
And whatever lies ahead
When I feel like giving up
I stop out instead
Trusting that life will come
I'll figure it out
Having faith
That's what it's all about
Stepping into the unknown
A few inches at a time
Holding on—
There's so much life to be found

Fields of Love

I'm running through an open field of daisies
Its fragrance fills my senses
Running as never before
God has pulled down the fences
I roll and laugh and sing
So comforted by the presence of my Lord
The wrapping of death is gone
And my arms and legs…?
No more cords
He has unleashed my heart
I feel so free and alive!
It's a pool of God's sweet love
I think I'll jump and dive—dive right in!

This Night

I'm trying to push through…
Is believing not enough?
Stepping cautiously
Through a path broken and rough
I try others' suggestions
To "make everything okay"
I try, but I cannot explain
The cycles within each day
Where am I failing…
What is it I have done?
I wish for someone else to blame
But…it seems there are none
I've nothing left to give
My own shortcomings have brought me here
I must find a way to work through
The uncertainty and fear
I pray, I talk, I read
It seems my biggest battles are with myself
It's so embarrassing and painful
When I have to ask for help
But there's a part of me still fighting
A refusal to give in
I desire to share my secrets
And the places my heart has been
A longing for approval…
To do just one thing right
Determined to find hope

As I look into this night
What do I do now?
I am so very afraid
I cry out to my God
But don't know the words to say
I cannot see my next step
Is there solid ground below?
I'm trying to employ
Every strategy I know
Don't give up on me…
I've got to find a way
First, I have to hold on
And make it through till day
The night stretches out before me
The path seems endless…
Longing for a hand to hold
Please tell me, what comes next?
If I keep pressing on,
What still lies ahead?
If I could believe
Are there better days instead?
I'm trying to believe things will change,
To have faith in my heart
Someone show me the way
I want to make a fresh start
I'm sorry I have failed
God, help me to be all I should be
Help me to understand
More than what I can see

I Push On

I'm finding hope
For my burdened heart
The thoughts binding me
Are falling apart
Having faith
For whatever may come
Each hour I live
Is another war won
Doing more
Than just getting by
Breaking through
All the questions why
Finding peace—finding hope
A new strength within
Moving beyond
The dark places I've been
I believe
There is real life ahead
When fear hits my heart
I push on instead
It's a new start
It's a new day
One day at a time
I'm finding my way

I Will Not Hide

I call out to my God
Another day has passed
I feel a little confused
Yet a sense of hope still lasts
I'm growing
I'm changing inside
I'm not proud of everything
But I refuse to hide
I bring to Him my fears
The pain deep in my heart
The secrets in my soul
That rip my faith apart
I bare all
All the good—all the bad
The things that bring me joy…
The things that make me sad
My biggest battles
Seem to be with myself
I feel I don't deserve His care
But He knows me so well
He brings me hope
When I feel I can't go on
Every dark night
Somehow becomes a dawn
I make mistakes…
Sometimes it breaks my heart
But there is a future…

Strongholds are coming apart
I have hope for life
I believe
I don't know the way…
But I will let Him lead
This is just the beginning…

Breaking Through

This morning I found
A hope that is new
In the midst of despair
The light's breaking through
Circumstances
Overwhelm and confuse
But finding
God's promises are true
He has brought to me
A song of peace
Believing in more
Than what I can see
Faith is not always easy
But pushing on—
I'm breaking free
No matter what I feel
There is hope in my reach
Growing and becoming
All I can be
Anything is possible—
I believe!
Looking ahead
It's a new world I see

New Beginnings

I have come so far…
But still far to go
Light at the end of the tunnel
Has caused my faith to grow
New paths and new directions
Appear before me now
I want so much to change
But still not always sure how
It's a day of new beginnings
Though the nights at times seem long
Less time given to tears
I feel myself becoming more strong
I'd like to share my faith with others
Of God's mighty, wondrous hand
Of a forming, stalwart will
That is helping me to stand
This time of beginnings
Takes my breath away
It is precious and dear to my heart
As I take on each new day

Crying Out

In the midst of despair
So very afraid
Crying out to my God
I can't find my way
Desperation
Has consumed my heart
Trying to work through it
But don't know where to start
Pushing on—
What do I do?
I cannot find hope
And options seem few
I feel so overwhelmed
It's difficult to breathe
Nothing seems to help
Don't even know what I need
God, help me please—
It feels impossible
I'm trying so very hard
Trying everything I know
Please, God, bring hope
To this turmoil, I'm in
Bring relief to the torment
And help me to live

No Matter What It Takes

My spirit cries out—
Where do I stand?
I've fallen so short
Of the life I had planned
Anxiety encompasses
My entire being
Overwhelmed by the battles
Each day brings
I'm at a loss…
What am I doing wrong?
Trying so hard
To have faith and be strong
Confusion eats
Through my spirit's core
It's so hard not to give up
Hard to fight anymore
But deep inside
There's a tiny flicker of hope
Though I don't know how to grasp it
Or which way to go
But I'm trying to believe
There are better days ahead
Even though I've lost strength
And my Faith is all but dead
I may bend—
But I won't break
No matter what it takes

A new step is painful
I'm unsure what to do
But one moment at a time
I will push through
Nothing is impossible
If I can just believe
There's so much I long to do
And so much I want to be
If I choose life
Then that's reason enough
I will put my trust
In my God above
One day at a time
One step to the next
As I surrender my fears
I'm finding rest
I pledge today
With all of my might
I will push on
Never give up the fight
Trusting my life
In God's strong hands
Using coping strategies
And developing a plan
I am excited
With these words I have said
Moving on
There's so much life ahead

Afraid to Trust

I'm truly at a loss…
Where do I go from here?
I'm so overwhelmed
With desperation and fear
I fight with all my might
I don't know where to turn
Doing my best to use
The strategies I've learned
Words cannot express
The despair that I feel
Struggling with myself
To be sure of what is real
I hate myself so much
I feel that I deserve pain
A drive to sacrifice
That's more than I can begin to explain
My thoughts are so jumbled
My feelings hit such extremes
I'm longing to find
The comfort that I need
See, if I hurt myself
Maybe if I really paid
I could forgive myself
And find the peace that I crave
I'm letting people down
By struggling so much
I want to tell someone where I stand

But I'm afraid to trust
I believe in God
But I'm just as afraid to trust Him
To believe that someone loves me…
How do I begin?
I'm afraid of my next breath
God, I'm crying out to you
If there is some way out of this
Please show me what to do

One Step

One thing I've learned
Over the long painful years
Life is what I believe deep within
Life is not what I feel
Memories torment
Despair and panic come and go
Emotions rage…
It's difficult to feel in control
But somewhere in my heart
I believe
That in my God and in my spirit
I can find the strength I need
I try so hard to hold onto
The often brief moments of peace
I feel beaten down
But there's so much I can be
I have hope…
Flicker though it may be
If I choose to believe
I can make it through this day
I believe as time goes by
I will grow stronger in my soul
I will learn how to feel joy
Gradually becoming whole
Today is a new day
I'm stepping out again
I may not be where I want

But so much better than where I've been
I choose to believe
One foot in front of the other
Moving forward
One step will follow another
That's it!
I believe…
I believe in life
Sometimes may be difficult
But I will never cease to try

Easter

The reality of my Jesus
It is difficult to conceive
At times, hard to comprehend
But I choose to believe
God has changed my life
He has rescued me
Though I sometimes struggle with doubts
It's so much more than what I see
I have lived though many hurts
But He is with me through the pain
When I think I cannot go on
His blessed new hope reigns
I come to Him humbly
Longing for His peace
When I feel confused
And my fears will not cease
It's then that I find hope
An amazing joy within
Looking at what is to come
Not where I've been
God's love is boundless
The very essence of life
The reality of my Lord
Cannot be denied
I pledge my heart
To do more than what I simply say
I surrender my thoughts and feelings

Learning with each new day
I love my God
With my very breath
Pressing on…
There is much more life ahead
Thank you, my dear God
For all you've done for me
Healing the pain of confusion
Setting my spirit free
This is a new beginning
A new day
A step at a time
I am finding my way

Surviving

My heart is heavy
But I cannot cry
The moment feels impossible
But I will not cease to try
I do not understand
All that's going on
I want so very much
To have faith and be strong
I bring to God
My wounded heart
And the harassing demons
That are ripping me apart
I'm confused and afraid
Struggling deep within
Searching for hope…
Where do I begin?
It's difficult to trust—
To share what's going on inside
To share my secrets…
It's tempting just to hide
Trying—
Trying to push beyond
Believing—
That soon will come the dawn
Taking chances—
I know I must manage my distress
But right now
I'm more afraid of life than I am of death

It's Not Real

Confused by trauma
Stirred up inside
Long to close my eyes—
Curl up and hide
How do I escape
The hands touching me...
It's happening again
How do I break free?
The physical
Is only half of the pain
The feelings inside fall
In an icy, taunting rain
I feel it in my body
How do I make it stop?
I want to believe I am innocent
But somehow I cannot
It's not just what my body lives
It's a gripping in my heart
I feel I am being raped
It's ripping me apart
Gayle—it is not real
Stop—please hear my words
The pain is tormenting
My spirit aches and burns
It is not happening
You are safe—it is okay
Reign in your thoughts somehow

We've got to break away
This will pass, girl—
It is not real
It is not real
The things you feel
Hang on
Despite how it feels
Hang on—
It is not real

I Stumble

Where do I begin...
Sharing what I feel?
I experience things
I'm told simply are not real
My heart feels tormented—
My body feels such pain
The violation of my spirit
Words cannot explain
Others don't hear or see,
So I try to reason it away
I choke on my own breath
Why can't I find the path today?
I creep—I crawl
Trying to break through the wall
Each time I think I have a grip
I stumble and fall
I don't know what to believe...
My thoughts are so confused
I'm searching—longing—for peace
But I don't know what to do

Shout

Dear God,
I need you,
Like the rose craves the morning dew
Like the field cries for the rain...
A promise of life anew
I love You
And I'll shout it from the mountain tops!
With all that is within,
Sing it out and never stop!
Like an oasis in endless desert
Mercy flows into sparkling cascades
Immersing me in Your boundless love
As You joyfully lead the way
Your creation spreads before me
In its splendor of heavenly hues
Hold me close to Your heart, dear Jesus
So I can boldly sing the news!

Winter Night

The sky is filled with majesty
On this crisp, cool winter night
The silence is unbroken
As sweet, sweet peace
Finds its way to my hungry soul…
Edging into my spirit
And making my faith fresh and real
Trusting what the mountains that I face inside
The oceans will wash away
My hope overflows
Some treasures of life I feel
I can never speak
Grace floods my heart
Day by day—becoming complete

Uncertainty

I don't understand where I'm at—
What is going on inside
I long to find a dark place
To curl up and hide
There's overwhelming desperation
In my spirit and my soul
A drive to harm myself—
Impulses are taking their toll
But there is a part of me
That refuses to give in
Trying to separate the present
From the places I have been
I cannot give up—
Thought it feels there is no way out
Trying to come to terms
With my confusion and my doubts
I want so much to be strong
And not let everyone down
I'm embarrassed by
The uncertainty right now
I don't know what to do
I don't feel in control
My spirit feels as though
I'm in a deep and swirling hole
I'm afraid…
What comes next?
I promise to keep fighting—

To do my very best
I have to believe—to hope—
I will keep pressing on
I believe there are brighter days to come—
I will fight until the dawn

Pressing On

I don't know
Which way to turn...
Trying to hold on
To all that I have learned
Don't really understand
What is going on...
But I'm working hard—
Trying to be strong
I'm fighting impulses...
Struggling for control
Laying down my heart...
Longing to be whole
My feelings change so much
From one moment to the next—
Trying so hard
To find my spirit rest
My thoughts get jumbled—
Uncertain and confused
But some moments God brings
A peace that is fresh and new
It jumps back and forth
As faith I work to grasp
I'm trying to maintain
In a way that will last
I believe...
In what lies ahead—
Not in the past

But what is to come instead
I'm moving forward
Pressing on
Pushing to believe
That soon will come the dawn

I Found Hope

My life is changing…
Day by day
I will not give up—
I'm finding my way
There actually is hope
And a sense of peace
There is life
That goes beyond my need
So many times
It seems I've reached the end
But I am stepping out…
Ready to begin again
I am sorry
If I've let others down
But I will hold onto
The spark of life I've found
The battle rages
What do I need?
Why now…
Why this hint of peace?
My next step?
I may not know…
But somehow—
My faith has grown
I believe
In what is yet to come
I may have made mistakes

But I am far from done
I lift my head—
God has brought me hope
I can do this…
I can do this…I know
Pressing forward—
One step at a time
I may fall…
But there's life yet to find

Mom's Birthday

Dear Mom,
I know life is full of changes
And the future can't be seen
But it is such a blessing
To have you here with me
Your encouragement and support
Help me to face another day
I go through many struggles
But I'm slowly, surely finding my way
Your friendship is a gift
That brings comfort to my heart
If I haven't spoken my love
I think it's time to start
At times, I misunderstand you…
And it brings me pain within
But a little at a time
You teach me how to laugh again.
I pray I'm also
A friend to you…
Helping you with
All the pain you go through
I think we help each other
Walking side by side…
The moments of joy,
And the moments we cry
It's a friendship that will last
For all eternity

It grows with each day...
And you mean the world to me
Happy seventy-second birthday, Mom—
I love you

Tonight

I drew strength from somewhere
Deep within today
So excited that
I can't find the words to say
It's coming together,
Falling into place
Issues, I'm feeling
More ready to face
There are people who care—
I see their hands reach out
I'm struggling to break through
My own self-doubts
I'm not sure what lies ahead,
What each day has in store
But I'm making new steps,
Opening doors…
I feel more comfortable
With myself tonight
Feelings push
To continue to fight
I'm learning more about myself,
My own mind and heart
Over and over—fresh starts

Birth

I don't really understand
This place I'm in
Fighting against
All I've ever been
Moving from being a victim
To a brand new world
It's as though I'm in labor
Looking at upcoming hidden turns
Which do I take?
I make ready my heart
For I know not where I'm heading
But I know I've made a start
The labor brings life
I control my breaths as best I can
I know deep within
I am in God's strong hands
I must admit,
I'm a bit cautious
It's beginning to seem
It's going to take a lot of trust
The fear that fuels my thoughts
And tries to dissuade the hope of my heart—
That fear is losing the battle—
The cords of confusion are coming apart

Changes

Things are changing
There are brighter days to come
Though I struggled today
It's another battle won
One day at a time
I am pressing on
Hanging on in my spirit
Until the hopelessness is gone
Though I may not know
All the answers I need
I am moving toward
Possibilities I see
A life of hope
Living by faith
Learning and growing
Every day's a new day
Finding life
In ways I did not know
Every struggle
Is another chance to grow
Looking forward
To the life that lies ahead
Pushing through the turmoil
Finding peace instead

Memory

It slams into my mind...
Memories—times past
I struggle to gain peace,
But it seems to never last
It's not just the thoughts...
There's physical pain as well
With it comes such shame—
Words simply do not tell
Will I ever come to terms with
The turmoil that I feel?
It feels like it is happening...now
It seems so very real
Acceptance...
What does that really mean?
When I look at myself
I feel tainted, so unclean
I pray for healing...
I don't understand what's within
It feels like
It is happening all over again
How do I separate
The present from where I've been?
I don't understand myself...
I don't know who I am
I come to my God...
And I'll trust Him

Free from the Maze

It's amazing how
In the depths of despair
My God brought His
Tender and healing care
Touching the hurt
Deep in my heart
helping me stand
And make a fresh start
I did not understand
What I was going through
So many doubts—
Not sure what was true
But God took my hand
And pulled me free
In my time of confusion
And overwhelming need
He showed me how
To use step by step skills
strengthening
My motivation and will
My heart is light
My spirit is strong
He has blessed—
Gave my soul a new song
God will help me
More than make it through
Free from the maze
This day is new!

Take My Hand

Sweet, little girl,
Take my hand
Try to be
As strong as you can
I know
You've been violated again
My heart breaks
For the places you've been
I see you try to stand
Shrouded in shame
I need you to know
You're not to blame
The guilt that
Consumes your soul
The deep, dark
Overwhelming hole
It's not yours—
We've got to break free
Your heart—your pain
It is still me
Sweet, young lady,
Take my hand
Try to be
As strong as you can
Betrayed by
Those whom you trust
Hard to break the chains

But somehow we must
Because of the past
We did not know
Where lines are drawn
Where did my innocence go?
So confusing
I know you feel so unclean
But you did not deserve
The pain you have seen
Fifty years old
Someone take my hand
I want to be
As strong as I can
Rapes have broken my spirit
Rapes have wounded my soul
I turn to every side
Please—which way do I go?
Overpowered
I cannot breathe
Searching deep within
I cannot find me
I'm trying to trust—
Another wall just fell—
I've begun to share
My own secret hell
It hurts deep inside
So many questions why
But I'm stepping forward
Trying to reclaim my life
I want to tell
The me I once was

Hang on—
We will rise above
I want to be able
To forgive myself
To feel the freeing hope
Words simply do not tell
Just looking in the mirror
Is a difficult task
I see all I am not
And every moment of my past
Press on, little Gayle,
Press on, young Marine,
Press on, adult woman,
There are better days to be seen
One day at a time
Working hard to break free
Searching to find
The new Gayle that is me

Dear God, It's Me Again

I do not understand, God
But I am trying to believe
The battle is so intense
Where is the faith I need?
I question my own existence
I question what is real
Somehow help me conquer
This desperation that I feel
It's so very overwhelming…
My heart cries out to You—
One moment at a time—
That's all that I can do
I was feeling so much better…
More at peace with myself
A matter of hours
And thrown right back into hell
I cannot allow myself to believe
The voices—all the lies
I'm trying to remember
You're right here at my side…
My spirit aches
From the voices and the thoughts
I know that you know, my God
How very hard I've fought
Please accept my prayer
Help me find peace of mind
I'm trying to have hope…

Not be the quitting kind
As much as I may long, at times,
To throw it all away
I'm struggling to be strong
And defeat that need to pay
You've brought me this far...
And I believe in You—
You're at work in my life
Even when I haven't a clue
In a matter of a few seconds
My world gets turned around
Images that torment...
Sensation...sounds
I will keep on fighting—
For you've given me hope again
I trust you to redeem my soul
From the places I have been

For Nathan and Annie

You are about to undertake
The most glorious of tasks...
It is a blessing far beyond
Anything you could ever ask
A child is a gift
Borne deep within the heart
The miracle of life—
Here is where it starts
The greatest responsibility
Lays within your hands
Rise to this moment
Rise up now and stand
There is no greater honor
Than your child's first smile
Take him by the hand
Step by step—mile by mile
The journey you've begun
Will challenge you every day
But also brings more joy
Than words can even say
Trust in the Almighty
Allow Him to lead the way
Pressing on to all that's ahead
Every day's a new day

Finding Reality

I want to make some changes
But I'm not sure how to start
The pain that I've been through
Has overwhelmed my heart
Memories flood my mind—
With fear—can' see my way
Struggling for control
As I start with each new day
Flashbacks come
They're so real—so happening
My whole body is consumed
I'm working for the day I will be free
I'm working so hard
Searching for truth
Trying to believe
Is a journey that is new
Trying to believe
My traumas are not my fault
Somewhere deep inside
I hear a distant call
In spite of all I feel
A call to keep pushing through
Right now, hanging on
Is all that I can do
I will not give up
Until I reach the other side
Learning how to voice

All the secrets that I hide
There is hope
Even though I don't quite understand
I will step on
With every ounce of strength I can
Today was painful and difficult
Trying to distinguish reality
I believe there must be life ahead—
More than what I can see

Please Hear My Heart

I long to cry out
Don't know where to start
Confusion in my mind
Despair in my heart
I see and feel things
That I'm told are not there
Physical pain
That's difficult to bear
Demons torturing me...
How do I make it end?
The voices and visions
And physical attacks blend
They do to me things
I can't even speak
The violation—the shame—
Makes me feel weak
It want so much to be free—
Where do I turn?
I want to trust God
And use the strategies I've learned
I feel so alone—
Such pain in my heart
I want to believe good
But don't know how to start
I'm crying out now...
Does anyone hear?
Can anyone help—

Help dry my tears?
Please hear my heart
Please don't turn away
Somehow—help me—
To find a new day

Rise

Despite what I feel
I will not give up
I will keep pushing on
I will rise above
I have faith in my God
This torment will pass
Another day will come
This is not the last
My God will bring me hope
I simply must hang on
I will press on
Until the distress is gone
Voices—demons
Impulses to harm myself
The confusion and uncertainty—
Can't find the words to tell
But I believe
I believe in what's to come
Finding hope
Through till this battle's won

To Overcome

What do you call a girl—
Violated again and again?
You call that child a victim
What do you call a victim rising
Who lived a lifetime stripped of honor?
You call that woman a survivor
What do you call a survivor
Who has learned to find new life within?
You call that survivor a victor
What do you call a victor
Who works past all the shame?
You call that victor a lady
What do you call a lady
Who has regained her virtue?
Now you can call her Gayle

The Climb

Thrown about
Caught in despair
The pain in my heart
Almost more than I could bear
So overwhelming
It caused my heart to burn
Relief felt more
Than I could ever earn
A little at a time
He's setting me free
I came to my God—
Laid it all at his feet
I searched my soul
Looking for peace
Somehow some help
In my time of need
I let go of the hurt
And surrender my pain
I'm climbing out of the pit
That has kept me restrained
There is hope!
Breaking free from the chains
God brings life—
His gentle mercy rains

Five Minutes at a Time

Words don't come easy
For the pain in my heart
Trying to find the truth
Is ripping me apart
I call out to my God
For I don't know the way
Something inside must change
If I'm to make it through his day
I do not deserve
For anyone to care
Can I believe I'm loved...
Do I even dare?
Because if I believe
It will get turned around
And my search for hope and peace
Become so tightly bound
Confusion, fear, uncertainty
Brew in my spirit's core
A maze of twists and turns
And I cannot find the door
Is there new life to come?
I want so desperately to know
I want to move forward
Please show me the way to go
I will keep on fighting
I will not give in
I want to separate the present

Form the places I have been
I'm afraid—very afraid
But I choose to believe
I know I've made mistakes
I don't even know what I need
But I trust God to bring me life
Somehow I will find the way
Five minutes at a time
I will make it through this day
I still long for hope
And I long for peace
For a breakthrough in my mind
The confusion and torment to cease
There's a light on the horizon
I step toward what's ahead
I want to leave this turmoil
Work until my fear is dead
New Hope
My life is different…
I may not understand
But I know, my God,
It is brought by your hand
You have blessed my heart
You have touched my soul
A day at a time
You're making me whole
A sense of peace
Like I've never know before
In a spirit that has
So long been at war
Desperation consumed me…

Hope impossible to grasp
I could not face my future
I could not face my past
But you have changed me...
I feel faith deep within
Looking forward—
Yet accepting where I've been
There is life yet to come
New hopes and dreams
I'm beginning to believe
In what's yet to be seen
Help me continue to grow
Help me to believe
A little at a time
You're setting me free
Thank you, God

Rise Above

What can you do
With my doubts deep inside?
My heart aches so much
Hope is running dry
I'm so very afraid—
As the battle rages on
I want to overcome
Trying so hard to be strong
Fear and confusion
Can anyone see,
See my need?
I feel tormented...
How I long to be free
I know I must
Endure all that I feel
Somewhere inside
Is a faith that is real
All I can do
Doesn't seem enough
When I feel this despair
Help me rise above
If only I could tap into
The hope deep within
I choose to believe...
Help me get up again
God, I don't understand
Why it is so hard

But despite all my struggles
You've brought me this far
I will keep fighting
Though the future can't be seen
Teach me how to receive love
And reawake my soul's dreams
I choose life
Beginning to feel hope within
Hold tightly to my hand...
Let another day begin

The Stream

A stream flows gently
Into my soul
Bringing life
To these weary bones
Soothing scars
Deep within
Here now hope
And peace begin
A refreshing calm
Engulfs my heart
Blessing me with
A brand-new start
The destruction that plagued
My mind constantly
Is falling apart
I finally am free

New Breath

I may bend—
But I won't break
One step at a time
No matter what I face
Through the barriers
I'm pushing on
Despite the struggles
My hope is not gone
Some moments
I'm very afraid
But a new breath
Is a new day
Where does
My fear come from?
Sometimes so much hurt
My heart is numb
But I believe
In what's to come
A little at a time
Rising above
I'm pressing forward—
It's going to be okay
Facing my past—
I choose to live today
Never say "never"
One step at a time
Always—always ready to try...
Looking forward
To the great unknown

Forward

Stepping forward
In a new way
Each night
Becomes a new day
Walking through
A jungle land
Doesn't feel possible
But I know I can
I can endure
Anything I feel
Words from others
Help my heart to heal
I feel overwhelmed
Much of the time
But working toward the peace
I so long to find
I have hope—
I believe—
I know better days
Are soon to be seen

Im Bound

Voices, impulses
Right and left
Fighting with everything
Fighting my best
I try to explain
But words simply do not come
My spirit cries out—
My heart is hidden from the sun
I am really scared
What am I doing wrong?
I fight with every breath
One day can seem so long
Right now, there's no where
That I want to be
Demons torment my soul and mind…
How I long to be free
It pierces my heart
That I am letting others down
I try to move…
But it's like hands and feet are bound
What next…?
Please take the knife from my chest!
If only I could feel more hope
I could conquer any test
I do not understand the triggers
Or why I feel this way
Somehow, God, help me believe

That soon will come the day
I want to believe—
With my whole heart—
For the voices and impulse
To stop ripping me apart
I want to be
All that I can be
I want to have hope
The soon I will be free

Waiting for the Morn

I must not give up…
Keep my head in the game
I'm fighting my own self
It's the victory within I must claim
This is not the end
I'm frustrated—torn—
I must hold on
Until God brings the morn
There is hope—
I must believe!
"Never say die"
My unfailing creed
One step at a time…
I'll no longer hide
Impossibility…
That's what has died
I can do this—
I will press on
My heart sometimes fails me
But my spirit is strong
Here we are—
Another day
A little at a time
I'm finding my way

One Day

It's one day at a time
We have to believe…
Our heart will be free
And find the peace that we need
It can be confusing
But we are on a path
Grasping for anything good
For a hope that will last
There is that hope
There is a way
Little by little…
Day by day
We can change
This is just the start
Reach out—
And follow your heart

Making a Plan

I'm facing my fears—
Developing a plan
Trying to embrace it
The best that I can
With the help I've received
I'm opening doors
It is getting better—
Still I want more
I feel some hope
I long for peace
I want to be
All that I can be
There is hope
In the midst of the storm
Working to find what's real
Working through the pain that's formed
One step at a time
Each moment is new
Reaching out
Trying to trust others too
It is scary—
A real challenge within
But I'm pushing on
Pushing on—I will win

New Chance

A chance for real life—
It's a new day
A little at a time
I'm finding my way
More moments of peace
I'm opening doors
That somehow
I couldn't even see before
The path is unfamiliar
I'm not always sure
But asking God daily
To make my heart pure
So much I long to do—
Fresh dreams
Flowing from my heart
And my mind in gentle streams
Accepting love and support
From those who care
Learning to trust
Laying my heart bare
Sharing the secrets
That has kept me bound
Is creating within my soul
A new sound
A song—
Of hope—and even joy
This present moment

The past can no longer destroy
I'm taking back control
Working to move on
Struggles come—
But the hopelessness is gone

With Many Doubts

There's so much running through my head
I don't know where to start
A lack of understanding
That is ripping me apart
Struggling desperately
To know what is real…
Visions, voices,
And the things that I feel
Battling a drive…
It's such a fight
Believing that I must suffer
That I must pay a price
I feel I deserve pain
For my uncertainty
I call out to my God…
The pain brings me to my knees
I want to believe
There are better days to come
Pushing, pushing forward—
But how I long to run
Someday soon I will laugh
Someday I will sing
I'm clinging to the hope
Just a nugget of faith can bring
I've got to believe
Though right now I cannot see…
God will somehow bring me peace
One day I will be free

The Light

There's light at the end of the tunnel—
I'm reaching with both hands
Impulses, voices, pain
I must rise and make a stand
I'm fighting so hard with my spirit
I am searching for hope
Working hard to apply
All the strategies I know
This is not the end…
I will continue to press on
As the hours stretch before me
Somehow each night becomes a dawn
I have to admit I'm afraid
At times, it feels impossible to push through
But I cannot give up
There's a flicker of hope that is new
I must believe—
I must choose to believe
I must break down the walls
And accept the help that I need
I feel something—there is hope!
I will somehow move on…
I don't always understand myself
But I will work hard to be strong
I don't know why hope came now
It has so evaded my grasp
But I must take it with all my being

And break free from my past
I have been learning a lot
I am changing inside
I may not understand it all
But I refuse to hide
I'm stepping out very carefully—
Just one foot at a time
I know that ahead
Is the life I long to find
Another day is another chance
I will not cease the fight
Somehow deep inside I feel
It's going to be all right

Mercy Came

I felt all was lost
But mercy came
I may have struggles,
But I'm not the same
It is a process
I'm on the path
Even if at times
Hope struggles to last
Whatever it takes
I will do
Pain is familiar
But my faith fresh and new
I believe...
And I will walk on
Even when fighting fear
The hope is not gone
Pressing forward
Coming to terms with myself
Having moments of peace
In a way words cannot tell

Lost Track

I knew God—I knew my country—
I knew what I believed
And placed before me
Was all I could ever want or need
What happened?
I want the "old Gayle" back
What purpose do I serve?
I've lost track
Where do I go from here?
I can't go on this way...
The voices say I deserve the pain,
How much more must I pay?
I can't find the words
To express what I feel within
Somehow, help me please,
Help me begin again

Free from the Maze

It's amazing how
In the depths of despair
My God brought His
Tender and healing care
Touching the hurt
Deep in my heart
Helping me stand
And make a fresh start
I did not understand
What I was going through
So many doubts—
Not sure what was true
But God took my hand
And pulled me free
In my time of confusion
And overwhelming need
He showed me how
To use step by step skills
Strengthening
My motivation and will
My heart is light
My spirit is strong
He has blessed—
Gave my soul a new song
God will help me
More than make it through
Free from the maze
This day is new!

Running

I don't want
To be me anymore
Self-hatred pierces
To the very core
I don't know
What to believe
Reaching out
From my frustration and need
Being alone
With myself
Is a struggle greater
Than words can tell
Who am I?
What does it all mean?
Longing...somehow...
To be pure and be free
Shame and regret
Hold my heart fast
Unable to break from
My jumbled up past
It's bitter and confused
My heart aches like a child
I run desperately
Within my own mind
I do not know
Where to go from here—
Praying each moment
For forgiveness to be near

I Will Find Hope

My heart is broken
I don't know where I stand
Trying to block the flashbacks
With every ounce of strength I can
Anxiety grips my chest
I'm overwhelmed with uncertainty
Trying to push on
There's so much I long to be
Depression has lessened
But my anxiety builds more and more
I cannot help but struggle
What is it I'm fighting for?
I want so much to be strong
I fear I've let everyone down
My heart aches deep within
And peace cannot be found
Please do not give up on me
I'm working so desperately
To sort the questions within
The turmoil that strongly grips me
There's got to be an answer
I cannot give in
Pushing forward
I will find hope again

Finding My Way

Struggling—confusion…
My own self-doubts
But moving on—
hands to the plow
Finding strength
Somewhere within
A connection to God
Where hope begins
For so very long
I was held by fear
Many long nights
Spent in tears
Making changes…
I choose to believe
And as I do…
My dreams have been freed
God is healing
My wounded heart
I fall at times,
Yet make a new start
I will do whatever
It takes to move on
Battles sometimes rage…
But God brings the dawn
I will press on—
No matter what I feel
For the hope that I've found

Is precious and real
It seems that my life
Has new meaning today
A little at a time…
I'm finding my way

Changes

Things are changing
There are brighter days to come
Though I struggled today
It's another battle won
One day at a time
I am pressing on
Hanging on in my spirit
Until the hopelessness is gone
Though I may not know
All the answers I need
I am moving toward
Possibilities I see
A life of hope
Living by faith
Learning and growing
Every day's a new day
Finding life
In ways I did not know
Every struggle
Is another chance to grow
Looking forward
To the life that lies ahead
Pushing through the turmoil
Finding peace instead

New Hope

There is hope
For a better day
Making changes—
I'm on the way
Working hard
To let go of the shame
I refuse to give up
I'm not the same
Trusting God
To renew my heart
Sometimes heart and mind
Are so far apart
My spirit is becoming strong
Because I choose to believe
I'm asking for help
And beginning to receive
Desperation comes
But I will wait it out
I pledge to fight my fears
To fight my doubts
I may not know
All the answers today
But learning a bit at a time—
It's going to be okay

Beginning to Change

It can be so confusing...
Yet I know which way to turn
I ask God to teach me to apply
All that I have learned
I have to believe the good
Despite what I may feel
Even when I'm afraid
And I'm not even sure what is real
I believe—
In what is yet to come
Though I may get overwhelmed
At the race I've still to run
I will not give up
I trust God with my heart
I have begun to change...
This is just the start
Turning over my thoughts...
Sometimes over and over again
I cannot allow my present
To be dictated by where I've been
There are moments—
Surrendering the pain inside—
When I'm afraid and tempted
To curl up and hide
But I am reaching out
I am pushing on...
There are difficult times

But my hope is not gone
It's not gone
Because I believe...
I believe
In more than what I can see

Excited about Today

Sometimes I lose track
Of the path I am on
Times of despair—
But trying to be strong
I come to my God
Lay it all at His feet
He brings light
In my time of need
At times I fear
What the day will bring
Bouts of confusion
And doubts that ring
I may struggle
But this is not the end
I am in God's hands
And my heart is on the mend
I believe
In what is yet to come!
I'm moving forward
This day a battle won…
I am excited
About today
I feel more hope
Than my words can say
I even feel joy!
What is happening?
As I press forward

My heart just sings!
I didn't expect
This renewal
My spirit is free—
My heart is full
This very moment
Is a fresh start
Strongholds inside
Are coming apart
Moving on—
Here we go!
Stepping out
In this peace that just grows
I'm so thankful
As I face this day—
Step by step…
I'm finding my way

About the Author

Gayle is a former Marine Corps cryptologist. She is extremely proud of her service and looks at it as one of the happiest times of her life. She loves sports, dogs, and movies. She is a disabled veteran. Her poetry reflects her struggles and victories. She is also a comedienne wanna-be who loves to make people laugh. She is a proud mother of a son. She lives in the Atlanta metro area.

CPSIA information can be obtained
at www.ICGtesting.com
Printed in the USA
JSHW042327140721
16857JS00002B/3